Families can be made up of:

mums
dads
brothers
sisters
step-mums
step-dads
step-siblings
half-brothers
half-sisters
grandads
grandmas
aunties
uncles
cousins
foster parents
adoptive parents
parents' partners
carers
pets, etc!

Some

...but you can't live without them!

Blended families
(when two families come together)

Read on to find out more about how to enjoy great family relationships.

FAMILY

WHATEVER THE MAKE-UP OF YOUR FAMILY, WHETHER YOU LIVE TOGETHER OR APART, EVERYONE IS IMPORTANT AND EVERYONE HAS A ROLE TO PLAY WITHIN THE FAMILY.

Family life is about:

- Loving and caring for those people who are close to you
- Feeling safe and secure
- Considering everyone's needs and feelings
- Deciding what is best for the whole family, not just one person
- Being prepared to compromise
- Supporting each other through difficult times
- Working together towards common goals
- Sharing the care of children
- Spending time together
- Laughing and having fun

Successful family life is about...

TEAMWORK

Family circumstances can and do change.

Sometimes it can be difficult for children and adults when this happens. Talking about the changes together is a good way to help everyone.

How do I tell them I'm gay?

Will I cope going back to work?

I miss them so much.

I love my new foster family.

Our family is stronger since my partner and his son moved in.

Who will mum and dad like best?

I hope Dad's new girlfriend sticks around for a while.

Responsibility

Being a parent or carer is a big responsibility. It is the most important job that you will ever do. The rewards are fantastic, but don't expect everything to be easy.

Remember a child is for life and children need lots of your love and attention.

Always take responsibility for your **own actions**.

Don't just blame others when things go wrong. Ask the question, "What could I have done differently?" It may help you to see things in a different light.

Be **responsible** for your health and the health of your children:

Ciggies
Don't Smoke

Don't do drugs

Don't drink to EXCESS

MAKE SURE THAT EVERYONE EATS A HEALTHY DIET AND GETS PLENTY OF EXERCISE.

Teach children to take responsibility for their behaviour - but don't expect too much too soon. Children will need reminding many times before you can be confident that they will be responsible when you are not there.

Get your homework or chores done before going out

Practise good safety when out and about

WALK AWAY FROM FIGHTS!

Teenagers need to be given **FREEDOM** to show you that they are responsible.

But equally teenagers need to **BE RESPONSIBLE** to earn that freedom.

Let your parents or carers know where you are and what you are doing.

Don't switch your phone off when you are out.

TRUST

Trust is essential to good relationships.

Children need to be able to trust their parents and carers.

Parents and carers need to be able to trust their children **and** each other.

TRUST IS VITAL TO HELP CHILDREN AND ADULTS TO FEEL SAFE AND SECURE.

Always honour promises!

Don't make promises that you can't keep (that goes for treats as well as punishments).
Say what you mean and mean what you say.

DON'T tell lies!

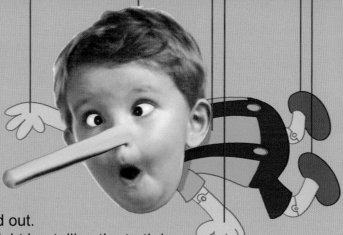

Lies always get found out.
However difficult it might be, telling the truth is always the best thing to do.

Lying to 'protect' children or other members of the family is never a good idea. The truth always comes out and when it does it's far more difficult to deal with than hearing it at the time from someone you love and trust.

Be honest with your children and they will be honest with you

Praise children for telling the truth, even if what they are saying is difficult for you to accept. Praise the honesty, then deal with the problem together.

MAKE IT A FAMILY PRIORITY TO ALWAYS TELL THE TRUTH

RESPECT

Respect is a two way thing.
To **earn** respect you need to **give** respect.

Respect the fact that everyone is different

Just because you do something in a particular way it doesn't necessarily mean that it's the only way!

MR. CHALK

THE TEACHER

MRS. BRICK

THE BUILDER

THE BAKER'S SON

Respect your home and environment

Respect others' work and achievements

✳ RESPECT YOURSELF!

Take care of your things and those of other people

Speak politely to each other

RESPECT OTHER PEOPLE'S NEEDS:

Quiet for babies to sleep.

Tolerance for overworked parents or students.

Privacy for teenagers.

Care for the sick and injured.

Assistance for those with special needs.

Patience for children (and grown-ups) learning new skills.

Time and space for those who are going through difficult times.

And remember:

Always treat others as you would like them to treat you.

Together Time

Make time for each other. Your time and attention is far more important than expensive toys and designer clothes.

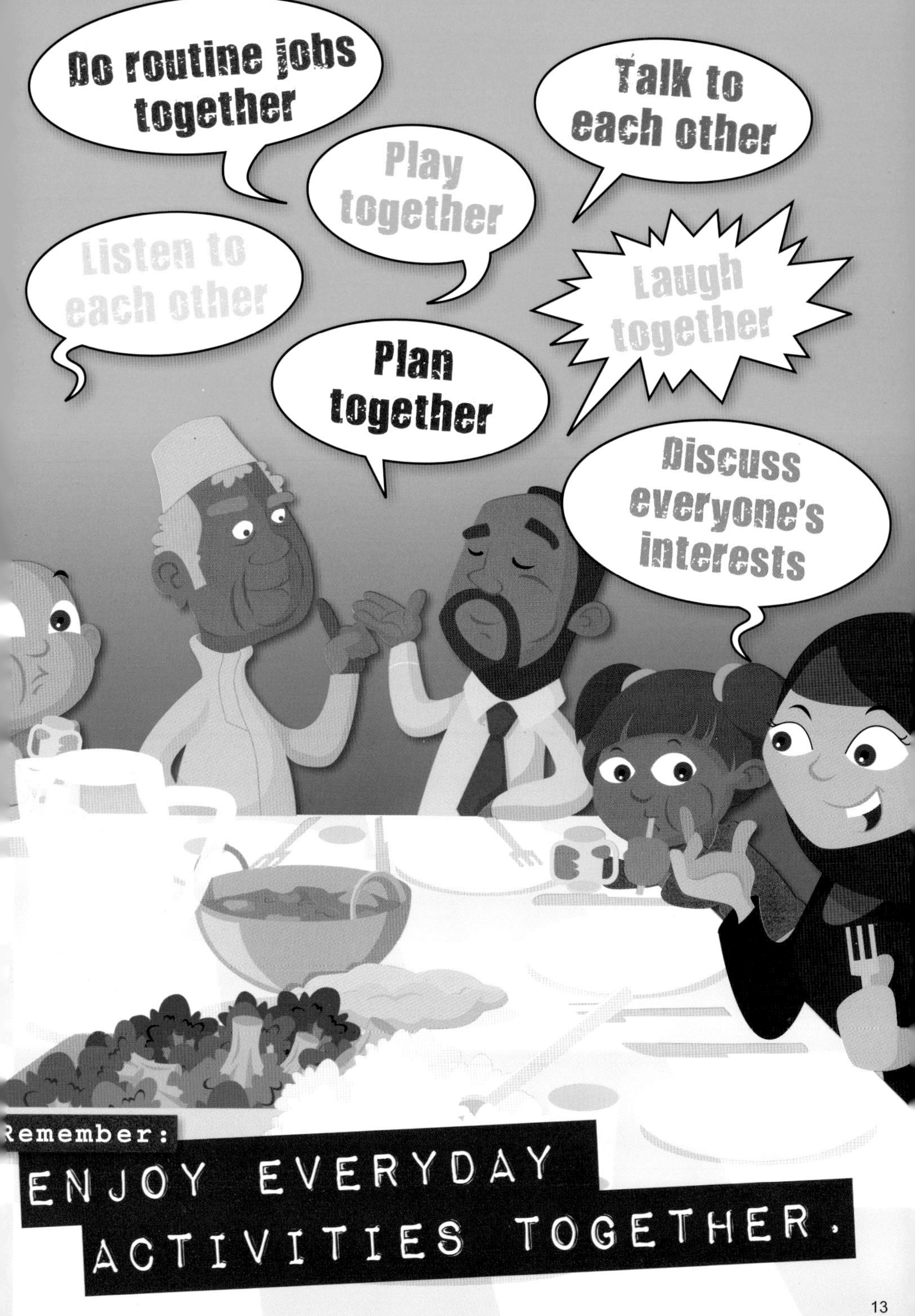

Remember:

ENJOY EVERYDAY ACTIVITIES TOGETHER.

Caring & Sharing

> MY LITTLE BROTHER IS GREAT FUN!

Understanding when others are upset or hurt

Sharing space!

Single Parents

It's important and valuable for both parents to share childcare and be involved in their children's lives.

Helping with homework

Caring about the needs of others

Helping out in times of need

Sharing chores

THAT'S MY EMAIL ADDRESS GRAN, NOW WE CAN KEEP IN TOUCH WHEN I'M AWAY.

Sharing Laughter

Some members of the family may have special needs and require more time and attention than others. It's important to help children to understand this, but also equally important to make sure they get special time too.

Sharing Problems

SHARING TOYS AND THE REMOTE CONTROL!

BEING THERE FOR EACH OTHER.

BOUNDARIES, RULES AND ROUTINES

Everyone feels safer and more secure if they know what's happening.

Having routines that everyone follows is a great way to improve daily organisation and cut out unnecessary arguments and problems.

If mum says no ask dad!

Even if parents don't live together it's important that they agree on the care of their children. This avoids them playing one parent off against the other!

Giving in to children to make them think that you are a better parent is not a good idea! It might deal with the immediate situation, but will cause more problems in the future.

Don't make rules that nobody can keep or boundaries that are unrealistic.

Families should sit down together and decide what routines and rules will work best for their circumstances.

Parents and carers need to guide children and help them to understand why particular rules or boundaries are necessary.

Tidying toys

Time to be home

Establishing new routines might be difficult at first, but persevere - the long term benefits will be worth it.

Preparing for school

Bathtime...
storytime...
sleeptime...
sweet dreams...

A set bedtime routine will help children to sleep better and will give adults time for themselves in the evening.

Be consistent.

ARGUMENTS

No family is perfect

Every family has problems

Every family argues

Try not to sulk, scream, shout or get violent - this goes for adults as well as children - it only makes matters worse.

And remember, children will copy adults' behaviour!

Arguments can be resolved more easily if we take the time to **listen** to each other and try to understand why the other person is angry or upset.

Don't dwell on individual comments that people make when they are arguing. People often try to provoke the other person in an argument and say things they don't really mean.

I HATE YOU! LEAVE ME ALONE!

Be prepared to admit when you are wrong and say **sorry**.

ADULTS: Try not to argue in front of the children because they will worry about what they have heard.

18

DON'T HANG ON TO BAD THOUGHTS - FORGIVE AND MOVE ON

Sometimes you might feel so wound up that you need a good **scream** or cry to feel better. If this is the case tell your family why, don't just scream at them!

Exercise is a great way to let off steam and it's good for all the family!
Try to do at least 30 minutes of exercise every day.

Don't forget the power of **sleep** - disagreements are much more likely when you are tired.

Make sure that everyone in the family gets enough sleep. Some people need more sleep than others.

Try not to go to bed on an argument.

KIDS: Talk to a grown-up that you trust if you are worried about arguments in your family, or call ChildLine on 0800 1111.

Working Together

Working **together** is the key to successful family relationships.

Not everyone in a family will like doing the same things.

But supporting each other is good for everyone. It's amazing how much enjoyment you can get out of doing things that you didn't know you were interested in.

EVERYONE WHO IS INVOLVED IN THE CARE OF CHILDREN NEEDS TO WORK TOGETHER FOR THE BEST INTERESTS OF THE CHILDREN.

This is also really important for parents who are not living with their children on a daily basis.

Make time to talk to each other - problems often arise when people don't know what's happening.

Working together to solve problems

Deciding how much information to give children will depend upon their age and maturity, but don't leave them in the dark about what's happening.

Be prepared to **compromise** to find the best solution for everyone.

Always consider how decisions will effect everyone in the family.

AND REMEMBER!

Happy families think **we** not **I** - and this goes for kids as well as adults!

Children, and adults, will always pick up the vibes if there are problems. Worrying about the unknown is far worse than knowing what is happening and being able to talk about it.

SUPPORT & CONTACTS

MANY THINGS CAN PUT EXTRA STRAIN ON FAMILIES:

Money Worries

Unemployment

Sibling rivalry

Alcohol/drug problems

Disability

Illness

Problems at school

Domestic Violence

And many more...

The most important thing to remember is: Never be afraid to ask for help